George Kalamaras

THE SILENCE OF THE
WORLD IS A FISHBONE

SV
SurVision Books

First published in 2025 by
SurVision Books
Dublin, Ireland
Reggio di Calabria, Italy
www.survisionmagazine.com

Cover image: Detail from Terraced Houses frescoes,
Residential Unit 2, Room SR 27, Ephesus, Turkey; photo by
Carole Raddato

Author photo: "George and Blaisie," by Beth Blake

Design © SurVision Books, 2025

ISBN: 978-1-912963-61-4

for Mary Ann and Blaisie

Other Books by George Kalamaras

POETRY BOOKS

The Gobi of Was (2025)
The Rain That Doesn't Reach the Ground (2025)
Robert Desnos Finds His Sleep Medicines Beneath Bachelard's Floorboards (2024)
To Sleep in the Horse's Belly: My Greek Poets and the Aegean Inside Me (2023)
What My Hound Dog Is Scenting Through the Sloughgrass
Is a Way of Scenting Me (2023)
Marsupial Mouth Movements (2021)
Through the Silk-Heavy Rains (2021)
We Slept the Animal: Letters from the American West (2021)
Luminous in the Owl's Rib (2019)
That Moment of Wept (2018)
The Hermit's Way of Being Human (2015)
Kingdom of Throat-Stuck Luck (2011)
The Recumbent Galaxy (2010), with Alvaro Cardona-Hine
Gold Carp Jack Fruit Mirrors (2008)
Even the Java Sparrows Call Your Hair (2004)
Borders My Bent Toward (2003)
The Theory and Function of Mangoes (2000)

POETRY CHAPBOOKS

Bootsie in the Bardo (2023)
The Shoes of the Fisherman's Wife Are Some Jive-Ass Slippers (2021)
The Mining Camps of the Mouth (2012)
Symposium on the Body's Left Side (2011)
Your Own Ox-Head Mask as Proof (2010)
The Scathering Sound (2009)
Something Beautiful Is Always Wearing the Trees (2009)
Beneath the Breath (1988)
Heart Without End (1986)

CRITICAL STUDY

*Reclaiming the Tacit Dimension: Symbolic Form
in the Rhetoric of Silence* (1994)

Acknowledgments

I want to thank the editors of the following magazines in which some of these poems, or their previous versions, first appeared:

The Bitter Oleander: "All I Had Lost"

Combo: "Why They Don't Eat Meat"

Double Take / Points of Entry: "Eight Hundred Vultures Feeding on a Dead Horse"

Fifth Wednesday: "The Galaxies' True Forms Expand"

The Glacier: "Sounding Very Much Like a Mouth" and "A Spectacular Grievance of Inverted Rain"

Omega: "Good, Bad, Indifferent" and "Love, Lust, and Loss"

The Refined Savage Poetry Review: "Wrong Side of the Body"

Sulfur Surrealist Jungle: "Falling for Lee Miller in a Previous Incarnation in Which We Never Became Lovers," "Ghost Offering," "How Beautiful the Cut," "The Inconsolable Study of Iron," "Initial Me as You Would," "Were We Sad?," and "What Ought to Move Through"

Talisman: "I Refuse to Let You Plan My Past"

Word For/Word: "I Wore Monk Hair"

Thanks, also, to the following for reprinting or featuring some of the preceding poems:

Gallery 308 (Muncie, Indiana) for displaying the poem "I Wore Monk Hair" in the exhibition *Arts Kaleidoscope: Art, Poems, & Videos* (October 2–31, 2008), and for reprinting it in the show's catalog, *Art & Poems.* The poem was paired in the show with the painting *Fish and Lotus* by Jha Sarojini Johnson.

And I offer gratitude to the publishers of the following chapbooks in which some of the poems in this collection previously appeared: *Something Beautiful Is Always Wearing the Trees* (Stockport Flats, 2009), *Symposium on the Body's Left Side* (Shivastan Publishing, 2011), and *Your Own Ox-Head Mask as Proof* (Ugly Duckling Presse, 2010).

Great thanks to my wife, Mary Ann Cain, for our shared work and love. Special thanks to John Bradley, my most devoted reader. And much gratitude to all those who nourish my work, especially Eric Baus, Michelle Comstock, Steve Fredman, Ray Gonzalez, Juan Felipe Herrera, Patrick Lawler, John Olson, Paul B. Roth, Geoffrey Rubinstein, Lawrence R. Smith, Tony Trigilio, and Lisa and John Zimmerman. Thanks, as well, to Jim Grabill, who took my work seriously at a time when I needed it most. Furthermore, none of these poems would be possible without the yogis of India and the mountain hermits of China—past and present— whose quiet contemplation continuously guides my life.

CONTENTS

Mutual Maps of Loneliness and Ache

It Seems the Length of Our Words Wasn't Enough

The Elegance of Eelgrass

A Primitive Sadness Has Plagued Me Birth to Birth

We Wore Monk Hair

*Truth rests on the mathematical reeds of the infinite . . .
and the oracle is pronounced by fluid electric fish.*

*

am I not the soluble fish, . . .

—André Breton

*but the eels keep trying to tell us
writing over and over in our mud
our heavenly names*

—W.S. Merwin

The bones of fish seem like fish

—Eleni Vakalo

Mutual Maps of Loneliness and Ache

Sounding Very Much Like a Mouth

At that time I had been busy writing an autobiography of my years as a
fire ant in Namibia.
I had to get it right, as the book was only one six-word sentence long.

Plato once said that Aristophanes had been a musician. That it was the
music of the spheres that wrote his plays, not the playwright himself.
And Tolstoy was still grumbling town to town, walking stick in hand, his
torn sackcloth slung over his left shoulder.

I wish I could write each village whole. Resuscitate the dead.
I wish I no longer had things for which to *wish*. That I could be awake
while asleep.

Last night, I heard a bird stir inside me. A falcon devouring a blackbird
devouring a worm.
I recognized the words but also knew it was the Word itself that kept
drawing me back into a body.

I have lived so many times that I am tired of the old alphabets. Even the
Sumerian cuneiform tablets I finger in the dark. The inscriptions
pressed into my skin.
Here, breathe unto me. Your clay or mine? Help me carve the
undiscovered marks of a new, loving world order.

The Cry of Night

I have written so often of death that I am remarkably alive.
You have bitten off more than all the jellyfish stinging the sea.

You have said time and again that I am a fraud.
That the guinea grass in my gut has never been there to settle the air.

You extract a tincture of feverfew.
Tell me the eelgrass must bend. The migraines cease.

You bow before my altar of bees' blood.
Pray to the peacock feather, asking that all that is sinking in you might
  one day fly.

I'm not sure I can go on relinquishing a hollow-eyed plea for passage to
  Paris or Peru.
You fancy the creepers and fallen trees. Tell me Ethiopia is somehow
  east of Brussels. That the Belgian Congo must cut off its *own* hands if
  we are ever to survive.

What kind of weather would be best to stir the grass? To waken in our
  chest?
What time of day would we feel most confident calling night?

If in Coming upon a Word

Thus, I realized the journey inward was the only journey worth making.
I said goodnight to the kerosene lantern and walked away, but only in
    dream.

Sleep bones somehow multiply my mouth.
They hollow and singe. And breaketh inside me.

The swamp-dwelling marshbucks are as sure-footed as rarefied rain.
Why, I wondered, was the thought of Kalahari antelope incessantly
    crowding my mouth?

We found moth hunters who appeared kind—even compassionate—as
    they violated their prey beneath a quite beautiful moon.
Pin my mouth shut, I pleaded, *so that I too might finally speak.*

If you want to fly into starlight, you must first learn that the mountains it
    shapes are inside us, among forest rubble and rain.
If, in clumsying your tongue, you come upon a word, then you will
    finally know the bent of trees. The fractured road to sorrow.

Please, I said over and again into the mirror, *help me to dissolve.*
I spoke your name into it, then mine, then somehow both at once. And
    the moon exposed a pulse of pines pooling upon the ridge as if finally
    pleased with my plea.

I Want to Know If You Still Love Me (The Question of Being Most Human)

I felt the sky enter my mouth and dark birds emerge from my ears.
It's we who toughen the tongue and weather the grass, was all I could
hear, in *not* hearing.

We can rest assured that the sorrow we feel is real.
How Maurice Burton, the famed zoologist, kept bees as pets, the
housemaid unthinkingly throwing the honeycomb one morning into
the trash.

We might exile her to Gyaros or Malta, saying she never washed
properly.
We might sentence her to three years of having to listen to the
trombone, then two more to the tuba.

Somewhere, near the gallbladder, there is a forest of Asiatic bears and
squirrel-like rodents.
That's where the Chinese acupuncturist settled her gaze, telling me the
imbalance in my spleen spoke to my lack of creating adequate
boundaries.

I wanted to know if you still love me.
I wanted to be confident in writing my direct plea to the question of
being most human.

We can rest assured that there *is* no rest. That the drizzle of rain remains
a drizzle of rain.
That during animal funerals among rats, the grieving rats devour their
belovèd.

So the sorrow Maurice Burton felt upon returning home to a can of
burned bees was gut-wrenchingly bereaved.
Dark birds enter and exit our chest at will. And the anguish we feel upon
waking each morning is real.

The Hurt Inside the Hearing Urge

It sounded current and old at the same time.
This wind this wind this voice in my chest.

Nothing would stop. *Everything* would stop.
There was no elliptical breath. No purposeful pause.

Cufflinks in my shirt the shape of eels.
Electric streams in the mouths of the dead.

Jellyfish and manta rays. Their indigo primordial pulse wavering in the
   reeds.
Please me my mouth, the moths in my mouth seemed to say.

Hand me the lamps, I thought, *so I might see myself singe myself to sing
   myself clean.*
*Oh, the way of the wind is the way of the wind where whispers of wind
   in the trees fall.*

It sounded ancient yet whole.
Wise yet dumb.

Like every word that birthed the earth upon the ache and age of the
   throat.
Like wind inside the wind speaking ceaselessly the hurt I heard in the
   hearing urge.

Unrecognizable

It has been written over and again that slugs do not predate snails on
the slopes of evolution.
Think of it this way: The rafters of my farmhouse were alive with birds.

Or were they burrs? Cockleburs or burr oaks?
Seems as if I was most grateful for a wild turkey egg laid beneath the
porch.

Of course I was.
I had sat silent for a month, trying to calm my breathing, but no answer
came.

Then, in seeing the egg, it was as if there were splendid halls of sea
turtles. Peacocks strutting the grounds.
Court paintings and Mogul ponds sunk into the gardens.

The palace had nine entrances, representing the body openings that
bind us to pleasure.
Yes, the Upanishads describe the hazards of the senses as we dwell in
The City of Nine Gates.

I have forgotten too much, and too much has forgotten me.
Imagine a house you once lived in that does not recognize you upon
your return from months at sea. The wooden doors. The creaking
floors. The way the walls seem to hold their breath whenever you
walk into a room.

Mutual Maps of Loneliness and Ache

Yes, I was born from two mothers, the second being myself.
I bend into starlight, especially when a sentence fails, its holes opening
the night.

Yes, I was born of three fathers, the third the sunburnt body of a dung
beetle feeding on bees' blood in Gabon.
How could I ever fulfill a paternal destiny and drink safely from my own
well?

I began to take up sewing. I studied crochet. I took dance lessons to see
if I could hear my feet weep.
Cookies and cashews were out. Kale was in.

All the avenues became boulevards, became lonely alleys where I
fraternized with streetwalkers.
No, it wasn't sex I wanted—but conversation. True words born from our
mutual maps of loneliness and ache.

There was a collector who journeyed from Bolivia just to borrow a passel
of crows.
Each month he promised to return them, but all that arrived was a
parrot feather that mysteriously materialized in the bird seller's
throat.

Yes, I was born from two mothers.
We might approach starlight and its milky sprawl with an ancient plea.

There were jackals and hyenas returning to their dens from the nightly
    hunt.
I crawled into the space I *thought* was my life and examined their feces,
    the dung I considered my tongue.

And each word I spoke on the street unto this woman or that was the
    elegant lope of a giraffe that arrived and died for my sins.
Its guts spread out among excited yips and yaps. A community of
    whines, whimpers, and wails.

Initial Me as You Would

I'll tell you what hurts. Beetles burrowing into Japanese red cedar.
Porous lava rock absorbing sound. Certain lunar phases without
moon.
Lice are common among our ilk, as if we waited too long to plait our hair
into horsetail braid.

The influx of September into July even made the Kodiak Archipelago
seem to weep.
Otherwise, the fog of my passing sadness resembled moaning
movements of birds breaking off into rain.

And in Denmark, great migrations of sound struggled to free furniture,
which held a parrot captive in an armchair's green corduroy.
In other words, everywhere I turned things were stuck.

I'll tell you what sticks. This resin in my wrist. This sap of a word. Certain
birth sores I bore as I moved from Kawabata novel to Kawabata novel.
If I resembled a name, if I woke—thinking with chloroform—they might
refer to me as *Execute High*, or *Foregone Moon*, or *Simple Kyoto Rain*.

Please, do not call me *Bakadori*, "crazy bird."
I am not in too much of a hurry to feed.

O great teacher of Japanese bedlam. O master of how many lives I've
   brilliantly bled. Show me the stones I scorched into the sores of my
   throat.
Initial me as you would a soapstone lamp. A flickering dark. The inside
   scar of a star quivering *The rain in our mouths is but a temple bell.*
   The rain in our mouths can do nothing but rain—as it rains and rains,
   calling us home.

Love, Lust, and Loss

The fact of the matter is that the kitchen really annoys me.
Not the cabinets. Not the sink. That we build a separate room for food
   presents us with a human dilemma.

I'm not at liberty to hand over the hairs you've shaved away. They, too,
   must nourish me.
I adore the smooth underarm. A bit of stubble upon my tongue. I collect
   the hair and keep it as a talisman of love, lust, and loss.

The phone will not ring. Who might be trying to call?
So much information is always lost, trying to manifest through the bones
   of sleep.

There's dew in my step. A water lily in yours.
Take my hand. Initiate our mouths. Draw the bathwater, please, from
   the erotic parts of my brain.

New Year's Morning

The answers seemed to require questions.
It was suddenly a new year. We were preparing to move from the
    American Midwest to Borneo.

Most of us didn't discuss how our body hair weighed us down.
We knew that a hurricane was the same as a typhoon—they were just
    called by different names between hemispheres.

My late night Indiana walks actually took place in the early mornings.
When the rain-soaked raccoon looked deeply into me, I knew I was
    destined to forever only wear wool.

I absolutely adored the wind the way I worshipped the wanton mouth of
    a lover.
It passed into me and stayed there, murmuring words from the
    Maumee.

When we arrived in Borneo, we learned to read the stiff Tarot cards of
    the jungle.
Something was lurking behind the strangling fig card as it overtook
    agarwood—the perfume tree card.

In those days, my friends named me *Witch Hazel* and *Sago Palm*, words
    that healed yet hurt.
Every time they said my name, a new year would begin. Thus, the years
    kept piling up inside me, as if carrying banners of who I had been
    from an almost-purposeful past.

The Unending Journey

The great Ituri rainforest is a dark memory.
There was an evasiveness of ants that I found especially irritating.

Much had changed in our separately announced deaths.
My biographer was generally unapproachable.

There had been unusually violent poetry in my mouth.
There had been a whole series of bad weather circling our encampment.

Accordingly, four sets of termites had been implanted onto my path—
    just to disturb me.
Their industrious movements gave me an impulse to march back to
    Brazzaville.

So when we had approached Stanley Falls two or three trading posts
    back, there were assaults of recurring misery.
Our ant-bitten bodies provided pain only a Dada poem or Ubu play could
    resolve.

And so the footnotes from that lifetime said there was a woman, a
    perfectly pleated abundant white blouse, and *a very desirable
    reunion.*
And so she and I had plugged our ears with recalcitrant fleas and called
    the unending journey home.

Nothing We Said

So we neighbored each other with songs roughened by sandblasts and
    wind.
Rude legends of murmuring ghosts caught us by surprise.

A mile up the road, pale animals suggested hardship and strain.
Rivers ran through the crevices of our sleep.

As epidemiologists, we had been certain of the multiple years of our
    skin.
How we had been born again and again into layers of a human body
    perplexed us.

Our nostalgia plagued us.
Our nostalgia was Whitmanesque in the most Macedonian terms.

Cut through the breach of grass, the hills and ridges, with a sword.
Conquer the lifetime of our mouths as if we were approaching the
    ancient war elephants of Afghanistan.

I remember other lives burnt and burning still—mounds of termites,
    fleas without fur, packs of wolves frightening as a forest on fire.
Their coats were sufficiently soundproof. Even when we begged of them
    their food, nothing we said unto them could penetrate their stiff
    guard hairs and get through.

The Other Side

So we struggled through the rainforest as if it were a long aching.
It had fallen to me to salute the moth wings and thatching grass left
fluttering there in strict striations of moonglow.

I wondered why the male circumcision ceremony was called *the
problem of unrequited light.*
Why the Kikuyu who hunted elephants always walked north when they
searched for watering holes in the south.

I had been exiled from the word *excision* and could barely remember the
inside bleeding of a star.
There had been scars in there like musical notes gone wrong.

From our patch tents we could scent the end of things.
After three cups of pine-smoked oolong, our conversation was an
alluring pantomime.

Here and elsewhere there was a notebook in which I had collected all
kinds of things.
Teaspoons of sassafras root. Broken honeycomb. Parts of stars I
imagined to be true.

Who could carry a commitment to everything and nothing at once?
Wear it like a talisman? Like a pair of ill-fitting spectacles?
Who might look deeply into themselves and see the other side of the
world?

It Seems the Length of Our Words Wasn't Enough

What Ought to Move Through

Now we take up the examination of what ought to move through.
Killed by photophobia, part of me is squinting in every childhood frame.

I lived in water colder than forty-eight degrees Fahrenheit.
I fought alongside the gear bones of a journeyman.

I have been trying to get rid of portions of my life for far too long.
Look: There some resin of it has even crept into *you.*

You? As if someone is actually enduring these words, kissing me—as it
    were—on the burnt blonde fur of my baby-blurred belly?
We limp of it and blindly through this life.

Please, if you find the now-rare coelacanth, place it tenderly alongside
    the boat.
Praise its insides. Compliment the complexity of its bones.

Close-reined, little fisherboy dangling his pole.
Extract the hook from your mouth—I will wave at you, tossing you
    another line.

Another line? Catgut from the intestine of a goat?
Innards from a possum washed ashore by river rinse and drift? Glorious
    fishbone dirt?

Here it is: just seven lovely words.
There it just went: seven salt-ridden words.

Such Is the Play of Light Within Silkworm Ephemera

By some accounts, I left the body when I was a Taoist sea dragon.
Those Taoist love poems always portrayed the divine maiden losing her
   speech.

Our words stick in our throat, even as we propose marriage to each
   consonant and vowel.
It has been a long courtship life upon life to finally try to get things right.

Such is the play of light within silkworm ephemera.
Let's call the azure-gem from pre-Han times by its obsolete name. Let's
   say it was *smarged*.

Imagine our past selves not as smudged or smeared or even smirched.
Smarge this, I might say unto the world, *when you examine the
   centuries embedded in my chest.*

Place a pock of moonlight into a verbally enchanted sea.
Precious be the pelecypods with their laterally compressed bodies.

Yes, alligators were supernatural rain-bringers.
Driven by mating fervor, they bellowed from their bankside burrows—
   when the drenching monsoons came—and in their thrashing carved
   the clay of what was later to be me.

The Immortal Abode of the Nine Ancients

First, we gathered clean water and boiled our metal pots for tea.
Then we steeped the leaves, which we believed immortal.

The scarred part of my heart allowed the rain its birthright of sassafras
    and grass.
Not just my lungs were breathing. All my internal organs rose up to
    display the fragility of the world.

Yes, several of my friends had left the body: Alvaro, Gene, even the spot
    of monthly blood on the bed sheet.
The mountain felt less alive without these friends to stir and birth the
    earth.

Breakfasts became lunch. Lunches, dinner. The evening supper, a
    magnificent marsh swallowing the moon.
If we called the dog by cat names, would it rain or snow? Would the
    sleet in my mouth honor both, suddenly bowing down to sound?

If we did the dishes by eating an extra serving of rice, what shaman song
    might we sing?
Surely, in such cases, more than the moon is made of glass.

Were there eight ancients? Nine? Twelve? Thirteen?
We could count the hairs in our mustache, or *grow* one—instead—in
    protest to the immortality of the lips. The lips—so fragile—that
    continuously try to move us into the next world.

Evening Bell at the Holy Monastery

We had traveled in those days to Java, Sumatra, and Bali. Even to the
Gobi Desert.
There were feudal loyalties. And warlike men scorned the love of
starlight as effeminate.

All that we exposed were evening fires in our nightly encampments.
All that we smelled were the scent glands of certain rodents and bats.

Great caravans had traversed this expanse with bricks of tea, flavored by
evening smoke.
We had been told that to lose ourselves before the campfires was a way
of finally finding direction.

Then the sound of wind through the trees as if we had been called to
prayer.
Then the bending of willows in the shelterbelt as if the earth were
bowing into us.

Then a remembrance of pain as if all we had ever wanted was forever
out of reach.
Then a momentary rain. A little more wind. And quiet.

Regarding the movement of fire ants, we felt them in our sleep,
vocalizing our skin.
Regarding the demand for high mountain oolong, we felt obligated to
share what we had, even if it meant depleting our reserves.

We knew such a place as this was the domain of hermits, poets, and
   adepts.
Out here in the wilderness, the sound of our yearning was as profound
   as a temple bell. Deep as the dark the ringing of that bell might make.

It Seems the Length of Our Words Wasn't Enough

Presently, we came upon a group of Chinese hunters tracking deer.
Sure, we were in Ethiopia, but how could you decipher the time of an
    exact geography if it was the moon and not a watch across the wrist?

We left the hut of a cruel November. There was an irritable distraction,
    birth sores in our voice.
It was not unlike coming upon dough in the undercooked center of a pot
    pie.

You kept asking me the formula for discreet provisions. For a perfectly
    functional life.
You said I must surely know the tender places and how to make you feel
    loved.

I turned and reckoned a Japanese schooner moving through the Miyako
    Strait.
There were Asiatic sight hounds in the desert, displaced pocket watches,
    and the dry mouth of yet another too-familiar famine.

What will we do with our bodies when we finally decide to give them up?
It seems a shame to leave our animal selves behind in a bag of bone dust
    on a shelf.

How sad to discard the earlobe her tongue had so lovingly licked.
The chest hair that had no urge to wander the jungle. That felt the weight
    and strength of something she felt for in the dark.

Gorilla Hunt

So you want to go on a gorilla hunt in southern Kenya?
You hadn't thought to, until our dream-sleep merged, and neither of us
    could explain the other's noise, nosebleeds, and smoke?

I have been vanishing like an eggless midnight.
I have crept ahead of myself into the awfully ethereal.

The precarious vegetation around our camp gave us an entire village to
    investigate.
How might the bitings of flies, the secret thoughts of mosquitoes, enter
    our flesh and perfume our sweat?

The sensible thing would be to forget the venous evening instinct.
It might entail asking the giraffe the layers of emotional weather—
    nineteen feet up.

An inscription of religion merits an unmarked grave.
We must atone that our celibacy emerged as a historical event, and that
    our writing might be better read backwards in a mirror.

In the meantime, I had a voluptuous headache staked on a silver-backed
    seam between my placental and marsupial selves.
As soon as my eye finished the morphine of evolutionary drought, I had
    perfect monovision with which to begin the hunt.

You Wonder Whether Language Could Ever Bend Itself Fully

Then I awoke inside an unsettled sparrow in my chest.
There was a bleeding ulcer in my gut called *Life*.

The caravans had passed, leaving bags of salt and bricks of tea wrapped
   in burlap.
I could still smell the smoky fires of how I'd thought things would be.

How can a panther crawling through the badger blood of night suddenly
   appear white as ice?
How can the snow be rain be sleet be suddenly solid ground?

Where are the commas, the pauses in our lives?
How might we attain the body anew without all the past incarnations of
   regret piling up—frozen—inside?

I ask too many questions?
You consider my queries fraudulent and frenzied?

You wonder whether language could ever bend itself fully into a willow
   on the banks of the Kankakee?
We hold hands throughout this interrogation and somehow emerge—
   fully in one another's skin—on the other side?

If just once our fever broke in the gangways and not in bed, we might
   step onto ground solid as cement.
There was an air of people disappointed in their lives. By all they had
   said and how. They walked circle upon circle in the dirt. All they could
   do was return to the source that kept consuming them and finally try
   to live their lies.

There Was a Difference in the Molecular Weight of Each Species of Ant

Then we embarked for the Kenyan montane forests in search of the
spotted lion.
One thing was clear—there was at least half an hour of salt in my blood.

I knew if I repeated my name backwards, the vines and creepers on the
trees would retract, responding in kind.
I knew my journey from Nairobi was not worthy of such an immaculate
inscription.

I gathered every article on eel farming that I could.
Yes, the weather was electric. And there was a difference in the
molecular weight of each species of biting ant on our route.

Our train car had only been a temporary solution. It is impossible to
estimate the weather projection of a bush-stinging wasp.
That night, you undressed—suggestively—in the patch tent, slid open
the mosquito net, and doused the kerosene lamp.

This is one of the most astonishing adventures ever written about and
bitten.
How two people could swallow a wind-drenched moon in the stinging
leaves of a rainforest and manage to survive the mangled flood plains
of the mouth.

I Wanted to Dilute Myself

There was a startling wind in my throat.
Salmon stream in the underbrush of words. A stirring like moths in the
  silk textures of my tongue.

During the progress of removing a coat, one arm was free. The other, an
  egret thrashing on the riverbank.
There were fresh hazelnuts, slender cigars. A way of seeking the holy
  Word we had forgotten.

Was it the Word that had been obfuscated or our seeking?
Something was always getting misplaced, modifying this, reforming that,
  as it strained a sentence, trying to reshape the world.

Say it was ragmatical laughter.
Say it was rasorial hen-scratching.

Say the missionaries' pile of snails said more about the slow growth of
  religion than hunger for the exotic.
Say anyone could be accused of abandoning the primordial impulse they
  inherited from birth.

I wanted a simple life.
I wanted to know what it felt like to weep at the exact moment the
  weeping ceased.

There was a dust storm coming in from across the sea, bringing with it
  the stinging sands of the Sahara.
Please, if you bring me the scale insects, I will make the red dye from
  them myself—so that I might dilute the blood burgeoning the
  mysterious night wind.

Once upon a Time

Once upon a time, there was no time.
There was no King. No Queen. No sons or daughters.

There was wind. Trees, of course. Oceans. And a great primordial ache.
There were no words. No fingers pointing to the heavens. A sound that
    floated the word *poet* through the willows.

Then it was as if we had been born.
We grew into a human body. We walked around with our insides on our
    outsides.

Everyone could see the structural integrity of a gnat inside the body of
    night, a body of night that had somehow flooded the seas.
Everyone developed empathy for the sick feeling in the gut others of us
    displayed outside of ourselves like bundles of tree bark and twigs
    waiting to spark.

There was nothing to eat because we felt no hunger. Only a hollow place
    we knew needed filling.
There was no fire to burn our regret because none of us knew what fire
    was, though we were told it would one day come. And that in
    touching it, we would hurt as much as *it* did in the simple act of
    burning itself into a blaze.

Terra Incognita

Back then I often escaped the bitter French winters by going to Algiers
    with the composer Camille Saint-Saëns.
We would leave our mouths a port or two back, asking etchings of fog to
    thicken our hearing.

That was when he warned me of a deceptive cadence the rain held.
That was when he offered the firm view that Stravinsky was insane.

I had been busy writing a biography of Captain Cook.
My thesis was that he *deserved* to be killed. That one should never steal
    wood from a burial ground or try to imprison a chief.

When I told my colleagues the islanders had disemboweled him and
    baked his body to facilitate removal of the flesh, they said I should
    write a book about bananas and coconuts instead.
During that time, a thatch hut in my dreams kept being set ablaze. By
    whom or what I never knew.

So I approached the Algiers market as one approaches lovemaking or
    prayer.
If we retain the scent of our birth bag somehow in our body hair, it
    becomes much easier to flirt with a piano of the opposite sex.

Yes, I loved Schumann, Liszt, and especially Brahms.
Yes, Saint-Saëns and I even traveled to Munich together to hear the
    premiere of Mahler's Eighth Symphony.

I still recall how often I left him to his notebooks and went home alone,
    knowing he had developed specific musical notations for melancholic
    joy.
So many nights I heard sounds from an untouchable place inside me—
    thinking they might be Saint-Saëns's—remembering one life in the
    Hanging Gardens of Babylon, another with Beethoven in the brothels
    of Bonn.

A Darkness Therein

You say there is a centuries-old rain we inherit incarnation to incarnation.
You say there is an expected explanation belonging to the sticks, straw,
and even the mud of a hermit's hut.

According to the *Scripture of the Ten Villages*, the world is weary of
crumblings and cures.
Poverty is a sad thing; even the cliffs and terraced hillsides know how
easy it is to slide into loss.

Think of the dismal years where an unwashed annoyance was as dirty as
a distressing falsetto.
Think of astonishing costumes that many of us call skin.

Each lifetime, each body I assumed, only drove me further into a proxy
for a customary labyrinth.
Until I became worthy of serving the whim of an irrigation ditch, I knew
all would be piss and mud.

I went to the Food Co-op this evening to find a gluten-free brownie I
read about in the monthly newsletter.
I walked aisle upon aisle searching the shelves for the darkness therein.
For owl light in the long shamanic night. For something tender and
sweet that would cure my crumblings and not make me ill.

Notes from *The Epistle of Fishbone Seas*

Those were the days best described as Buddha commandments that
   could kill.
There was a packet of letters from Kyiv explaining horse care from the
   ancestors of Cossacks.

There were winter nights near the Black Sea without coal, blankets
   turning from sleep.
When we said our teeth ached, it was not a metaphor.

Sheep and poultry were as valuable as skiffs and fishnets.
Intercourse moved simply from lovemaking to a way of generating heat.

But is making love ever simple?
Even in confidence, in calm, we giveth ourselves unto the unknown
   release of starlight coursing through our blood.

We Saturn-turn and Neptune our belief that part of a word broken stays
   in the mouth. And fishbones sink into silence.
All the planetary oceans rise and fall in our brains, as our passion also
   rises and falls.

These letters. This packet. This horse lore of whom and what we do.
Winter could be a way of asking for the simplicity of a good story
   fireside with Borges and his grandfatherly cane.

Tell me, my brothers, if *The Epistle of Fishbone Seas* could ever survive
   Siberia and the cold breaches of the north.
Tell me, my sisters, if *The Book of Death* is a book about the self-
   immolation of birds or a lovemaking guide on how to stay alive.

The Elegance of Eelgrass

Eight Hundred Vultures Feeding on a Dead Horse

From Himalayan flower graves to the snowy mountains of Morocco.
From the mating dance of the Argus pheasant to the efficacy of my
   memory.

In less than ten minutes it will be picked clean.
Sometime, afterward, a woman—wrinkled and motherly—came to see
   me.

My mouth calmed at the milk sac of a Bactrian camel.
The weight and depth of a boulder calling up to me from the gorge.

It was the rickshaw wallah from Varanasi who first showed me the bones
   of the fish.
When I am dead, I might reinhabit the observation tent to study
   pheasants.

Because the griffon vultures of India once claimed my body.
Because my pubis was the first to go. Then my wrist socket. Then a
   thigh.

The dramatic effect of living in Indiana in 2024 and breathing.
The miraculous recovery of the body after a night's sleep.

The Studio of True Appreciation

Now we come to the practice of tea.
How some leaves in a bowl have little to do with scholarship on a tatami
  mat.

We come as totems. We sippeth and relinquish our mouths.
We accept that nonacceptance is a form of approval.

You keep asking if I've tried Snowy Mountain Tea.
Repeat that it comes from the region where the original tea trees of
  China first appeared.

You ask for a cup of fragrant air.
For eelgrass near shore to bend and bow with each tide pool set
  aground.

I have been odorless. I have been wise.
I have sipped and asked my mouth to burn off just one letter of itself
  into a most delicate moth.

You glimpse my face in a mirror, hear me repeat myself. Decide I should
  shave away the echo of my morning ache.
Your smooth underarm upon my tongue is enough to move me to quite
  unexpected tears.

When the tea retreat the Ming Dynasty painter Wen Zhengming calls the
Studio of True Appreciation makes itself manifest, our seventeen
ways of weeping fly into a sky of quite dead birds.
Of course, there were parts of ourselves left over in the leaves, in back
alley tea stalls and chipped clay cups, in contemplative tearooms in
forest retreats where in drinking the universe from a porcelain cup
we become most undone.

The Elegance of Eelgrass

She and I debated the elegance of eelgrass.
One of us, as a boy, could feel tenderness in the unfinished breathing of
    each fishbone.

Even if you mention a cruel mud flat.
Even if the fence constrains crows and crickets.

The clay pot of apprenticed conversations is an enormous secret.
I have spun the wheel and dirtied my hands many lifetimes just to
    survive.

What is it we search for life after life in the moist clay of another's
    mouth?
How might our hands? Where might our tongues? How would that most
    private scar which I extend with primitive ease enter the hairy cupped
    curve of a star?

You think me crude for saying such things?
You say I objectify the voluptuousness of the apple on the counter? The
    lay of my wife's hair across the pillow? Even the almost-face staring
    back at me from the moon?

A book of blood?
A book of blood rushes through the shallow gravel beds to fill my tongue
    with the gaps from my most secret mood?

Even if you swim toward me, my darling, and salt the fish to ward off
    oceans?
Even if the glue of our bones—as we lie together woman to man, tongue
    to tongue—comes, a moment, unstuck?

The Journey Inward (Body Time No More)

Quietly. Quickly. The sun sank over and over in our ears.
We required additional provisions—blankets, candles, and canvases.

We'd brought plenty of pencils but soon realized we had nothing to
write about.
We kept trying to write our name, but as soon as we got a letter or two
down, the wind would lift our lead inscriptions right off the page.

We knew nothing was going to work. That even our memories were
coming unstuck.
We set out walking north toward The Land of Holy Seeing.

There, a Siberian shaman had been waiting to guide us further into the
folds of evening.
He held in his palm a piece of goatskin containing black and white
pebbles and three drops of rain.

Honestly, we grieved that the day before was now buried in the long
years behind.
We knew we had nowhere else to go but home, but we no longer knew
where home was nor how to find it. Nor how to ask if it would even
welcome us if we were to return.

Why They Don't Eat Meat

He never quite realized all he had eaten.
The low-lying areas of well-developed calves, tongue-licked and clean,
  were an altogether rough feeding.

He's not speaking in three separate voices just because he's vegetarian.
Examine your posture and the urgency of your own animal stance.

There is an indeterminate hour when the passing of appropriate blood is
  expected.
Imagine a game of cards in which no one ever won.

He will search the sucrose-dappled bones of bees.
They might drone away the graphite scratch of the word *Tasmania*,
  gather in caves of Australian anthracite.

Around his Latin name was a whole series of bad weather.
He watched the development of his contusions all evening on the
  Doppler radar.

How embarrassing to wake fully clothed when he thought their passion
  had broken through the boundaries of their skin.
Say my cow name! Say my cow name!, he thought they had both
  rapidly screamed, until—cinched tight—the panting belly-burned the
  feed.

Our Way into the Mind of the Animal Is Bolstered by Cockleburs

Often, our way into the mind of the animal we eat is full of star-spurs
   and cockleburs.
We search for the dark *in* the dark.

To the Western eye, the lack of shoes is proof of hookworm and the
   purest poverty and despair.
We understand that an extravagant throne room contributed to the
   downfall of the Manchus.

Nonplussed, quail thicken the thickets, boil out at the first word broken.
Light is like that, always quarreling with the dark.

The shaman, though, understands bones of the dead as streams from
   whence the river came. Fishbones, especially, as a quiet calm.
It is like standing on an ice shelf and sensing, for once, the desolation of
   a desert bloom.

As the traveler races north on the Southern Railway, so my mouth is
   embedded in an ear of sea lice.
Whose ear remains a mystery, but when I turn to touch the woman's
   breast in the dark all the embryonic movements fall away.

You say I never grew up. That I am a disgusting case. Lustful. Lewd. That
   in my late-sixties I am still an Argonaut wandering the birth bed in
   search of the amniotic fleece.
Honestly. Please. Give it a rest. Don't scorn me for all the unread shelves
   in my house. The many bookmarks stuck in the early chapters of far
   too many tales of Chinese medicine, endoparasites that heal, and the
   hidden hen's teeth for which we plead in the dark.

Odysseus Dreams He Is the Sea

I have been told that this ache in my gut originates in my ears.
It was a war exile from Ukraine who first warned me of the potency of
   this weeping.

It was a willow by the river that first spoke to me in ways I could barely
   hear but somehow felt.
I swear, this body of mine this time—so temporary—has taken far too
   long to get used to.

We step in for a short while.
We step out for quite many summers.

There are elevators and watchbands and fleece-lined coats that keep
   calling me to stay.
These are the ups and downs of time. Of spending many years imagining
   I could stay warm with jac-shirts and cozy linings and a good long
   dose of sleep.

In a world cold enough to kill, we withhold medicine and food from the
   sick and hungry in the name of free-market wax and the burning of
   church candles.
We place light before the icons in the sandbox in the church's narthex
   and pray the small fires won't somehow spread and consume us.

When Odysseus returned from Troy dressed as a beggar, no one
   recognized him except his dog, Argos.
Did he want his wife after all those years apart? Or had he been content,
   imagining her to be the glorious blue sea rippling in his throat?

Icon of St. George Revisited

By bringing together certain gratuitous assertions, we encounter
    incongruous images manifesting the mouth.
Ask St. George who, on his white horse, was destined to save the
    maiden.

Sure, the dragon breathed fire.
But who among us has not lit paper and straw—and stood in it—in order
    to become more beautiful?

You refer me to a temperate declaration.
You insist that certain aboriginal tribes in Borneo acquire the power of
    stinging bees when asleep.

That does not mean that tribefolk *sting* the bees.
It means they learn to fly inside the bodies of certain tree fruits poised
    before the storms.

I am speaking about life becoming life. Death dying unto itself.
Forgive me my explanation, but I worry sometimes that in reading my
    words you might walk with a limp rather than leap.

Such explanations could be my own attempt to save the maiden from
    what's below the horse's belly.
Could be my propensity for believing I could save the world from the
    world itself.

The Hero's Journey

So I found a specimen of the bright green whipsnake suffocating a
   branch of the strangler fig.
All the hunters we encountered were strong and free of disease except
   for a cough some could not shake nor one we could easily identify.

Nearby, axes could be heard, and something cut deeply into me.
Someone had clear-felled a chunk of rainforest, and I wondered if the
   rain knew whether to return to that small circle of village or instead
   pass it by?

Someone was at work on a blowgun, standing near a pot of boiling
   beeswax.
Someone else had carved up a book, dropping pages into the pot, one at
   a time, each in turn from back to front.

So the journey back finally found a way to return to its source?
So a single page at a time, our lives moved backwards from *The End* to
   Once upon a time?

Was this an origin story of small birds rumbling out of my chest and
   entering the trees?
Was this a full-throated rain that came unto me, welcoming me back
   after decades of desert and a stumbling search for well water?

I kept hearing that poets should *find their voice*, as if it were somewhere
   out there in the barren territory, avoiding capture and being tamed.
I wondered how long mine would keep evading me. Whether
   domesticating it was even ultimately the right thing to do.

Yes, I reread the passage *Once there was a king, and he had three sons.* Yes, I understood that the youngest was a fool. That he set out from the Kingdom on a quest among creepers, vines, and many thickly lined trees. Just like me.

War Crimes

It was wind; it was rain; it was a slumping in the throat.
It was almost more than we could bear—this being human.

I heard sound from a far holler, just over the knob in Disputanta,
   Kentucky. I saw lanterns in the night woods and ginseng being
   chewed.
I heard death cries from Persian and Tyrian armies, Macedonian women
   in labor crying out on cots, begging for water and its release.

What is past is present? What is close is far away?
Salt and pepper in the brain, they say, can make us into an exotic
   seahorse. We fall into our male bodies on occasion and ache into the
   ocean thousands of vulnerable eggs.

I once took an entire year to study the paintings of Mario Prassinos, the
   lesser-known older brother of his more famous Surrealist sister, Gisèle.
I swear to you—it was like examining the insides of dying insects for
   flakes of volcanic lapse and snow.

This was neither good nor bad but a ritual that expected me to pour
   libation and recite a poem in the form of a dirge.
To play the dulcimer and washboard, say, in a remote holler from which
   centuries of the dead might stir.

I once trotted up a hill leading a battalion of Alexander's men with
   sarissas, xyston lances, and kopides.
I remember stopping halfway up, removing my helmet, and turning back
   toward my men—asking for water, begging them to go home and not
   follow me any further.

As If Embedding Our Names into the Skin of Another

We finally had to decide whether we made time or time made us.
I had been traveling again, that lifetime, in Ubangi-Shari, cutting back
    each creeper vine like tending the various weathers of my emotional
    landscape.

I'd propped my gun against a baobab tree, as if giving a rib. I peeled back
    a branch from which womanly courage might emerge.
I'd given away all my rice and cloth in Cameroon and Gofa. Hoping to
    redeem myself.

We had come to the continent with many questions.
We were obliged to ask ourselves why the minute hand was longer than
    the hour hand when an hour of time is longer in duration.

Sure, a stand of trees confused me. Were they aspens murmuring or
    spirit beings mumbling my noun-dead name?
Yes, we possessed a remarkable ability to open our ears and allow our
    mouths.

We interrupted our breakfast in order to remove bamboo splinters from
    one another's wrist.
We spoke low as if embedding our names into one another, without
    anyone else knowing.

After visiting four, maybe five, villages, we decided to dress in
    cummerbunds and Tunisian waistcoats.
We figured that if we could hide our flaws and control the way our
    bodies were viewed, we'd have a chance of controlling not just the
    wind but the world.

Beautiful Breathing

Then I opened myself to the transcription of your arm hair.
Listen to the wind-drenched voice of a raccoon on the banks of the
    Maumee and somehow manage the dark.

Each day I bite through the droppings of sparrows. Displace discharge
    from a stray cat's eye.
When the blood is distributed, I am first in line with my cup and quarter.

The saturated disasters of desiring human bodies leave us craving more
    of ourselves as old age code.
I have come again into a sort of life, this time from the moist mouth of
    the North Country to demand the return of the right portion of my
    left ear.

You say you have been listening for me for a long time. Through the
    hurting world in your throat.
Tell me if I have materialized as you had hoped. If not, I swear I can
    repair the leopard skin mat upon which you meditate cross-leggèd.

You hand me a bruise, tender, familiar, and say there are more
    hydrangeas where that came from.
I offer an apology for the miracle of my breathing that has somehow
    strengthened the trees.

Little dwindling time on this earth, I am dumbstruck with your
    intelligence.
In my hunger, I am unfit for an amiable rain.

Touch me with the exact shape and shade of an egg.
Hand me a gold hoop for my ear; tell me—*this* time, in *this* life—that I
   will never cry out. Again.

All I Had Lost

I dreamt a human chair and sat in its curves.
It had nothing to do with wind-billowed drapes. With moon-bruise
   shared in the touch of two sweethearts.

Then there was the knife through the sole of my left foot. Was I
   suddenly trapped in a Max Ernst collage?
To this day, it's my right leg that limps, as if owl-driven, sombrero-
   scented, and wise.

It you want to caress the ankle bracelet of your belovèd, ask with your
   eye if she might finally release you from her breath.
Do not clasp, grasp, or shift, at least if you want to avoid delay.

I dreamt I was going mad, that I lived life upon life, spinning in the Great
   Wheel of Confusion—that I was a man, then a woman, then a monk,
   perhaps a chair, a bed skirt, even a bit of bacteria or slake of
   confiscated salt.
It had something to do—I'd been told—with vast mountain passes and
   the ever-embracing cosmic sea.

There are many tales of mystery and imagination.
I opened *The Book of Iodine*, *The Book of Thirst*, and saw the shape of
   my name in Sanskrit script, in pools of Macedonian blood, in spears of
   Sumatran rain, as if I were contained in all the words I once uttered.
   And had lost.

A Primitive Sadness Has Plagued Me Birth to Birth

A Primitive Sadness Has Plagued Me Birth to Birth

So it was Carl Jung who engaged the primeval forest in a significant
discourse.
Ernst Cassirer gave life to a torch-lit cave on the border of Belarus.

I can count on the teeth of my left foot how many sounds I have tried in
my life.
I offer escape from a viviparous right hand somehow larger than my
toes.

You're puzzled. Say I should shut up once and for maybe?
Give in, that is, to a primitive sadness that has plagued me since birth?

If we remember correctly, both Novalis and Kafka had a strengthening
relationship with death.
Consumed by a cough that never quit. A thickening phlegm that
somehow and always.

I can't go on roaming these depths any longer unless Rilke assures me
his voice is embedded in the clarified air of sassafras hollows and
wood sorrel.
Like Herodotus beckoning me centuries before this birth, I am
chronicling the battles at Marathon and Thermopylae, mapped in the
palm of my hand.

There is an insignificant metaphor conjuring a wayward etymology as if
it were a burning bush.
When the entomologist cabled me from near the Białowieża Forest with
illustrations of what he had found, I feared the worst. Left, as I was,
all night to dream of old bones among the bleached and tenuous
trees whose slow growth came to grieve me.

Wind Within Wind Within the Way Trees Bend

All around us the moon kept on changing, speckling the Acropolis.
I was tired of returning. Month to month. Year to year. Body clay to
body clay.

That was when a little owl appeared. Was she Athena or just the way of
the world?
There was a stirring in my chest. Wind within wind within the way trees
knelt before the ever-rising river.

And so country living became more difficult.
What lay ahead of us was part of ourselves we thought we'd left behind.

Sure, there were clichés within the well-worn wind.
Yes, everything kept returning, including the worms of human
indifference.

So much was passing me by. Especially when I sat by a river.
I saw my reflection in the still places of the Arkansas and Colorado, but
they felt like Elytis's "Aegean Melancholy." Seferis's *moon that rose
from the sea like Aphrodite.* Even the monotony of the Maritsa.

I spoke English with an inflection of Greek.
I had serious *avgolemono* soup in my veins. *Baklava* in my ears. The
watery juxtapositions of Hector Kaknavatos's Surrealism in my throat.

After grasping for handfuls of burnt hair, I was certain I needed warmth in the frightening regions of love. In perfect Athenian adoration. Even in the uncertain yearning of Eros.

Having sighted the fat black coils of a great tree snake, I heard a rumbling in the underbrush of my voice, which stirred into a spectacle of *above* being *below*. Of the falling soil lifting up through me into the swift-moving rain.

The Silence of the World Is a Fishbone

Some said it got caught in the mouth.
Others, the throat.

Either way, it only came *close* to silencing the Hesychast from Mount
Athos.
He swore he had lived at least one lifetime as a naked sadhu in India, an
Aghori smeared in cremation ash, drinking from the rain-scooped
skull of the dead.

Lord help me if I ever return into a body again.
I simply can't imagine reliving all this pain—even the love bites, the
ebullient mice moist and manic in my bones.

I can speak directly because I already know you as myself. Sensing your
skepticism in my sudden seizure of rain.
I can imagine your 120-year-old pet parrot can decode a lost Amazonian
dialect that quite resembles me.

Then there was the lifetime I smoked hash and played bouzouki with the
great Greek *rembetika* street musician from Syros.
Markos Vamvakaris sang a song into me that said a name like *Kalamaras*
is often ocean-bound, melded with jellyfish, sunken into the lost
fluids of antiquity.

What little age spot of fear has manifested tonight on my wrist?
After my grandfather's melanoma, I learned to dash to the
dermatologist without pause. Even for just normal aging. Even for just
a toothache.

I know you're tired of the dislocations of my mouth. The vulnerable
   sensitivity with which I speak. With which my few stubborn baby
   teeth keep saying the wrong word, marking my skin.
That you'd prefer I talk in Alexandrines or even just rhyming couplets has
   been noted in the most recent edition of the *Oxford Guide to Poetic
   Flattery.*

The silence of the world is a fishbone, I heard the eels telling me, over
   and again in my perplexed mud.
There, the electrical impulse of living lived and died, lived and died so
   many times that I walked around in a human body—in this
   incarnation and that—thinking I was alive.

Equatorial Wrist Resin

Then I returned from French Equatorial Africa.
After just one evening with a woman of extraordinary intelligence, I
    realized it wasn't just her—but I was in love with being in love.

Don't mistake my desire as a patriarchal weather pattern.
Fierce and full of hurt, all kinds of storms keep hurtling toward us.

If a piece of thunder.
If hurricane winds.

If the palm-tree bend of her wrist.
If in my mouth but already less-fractured.

There are arrows in my heel. Wooden horses I crawl into the belly of.
    Fish bloated and beached ashore.
Starfish in the attitude of streaming out toward the untamed reaches of
    the universe.

I could count to five and never understand the four corners of my
    mouth.
I am in love with the act of loving. And it is only that, that is exact.

Please, if you find Dragana, warn her it's not just the lay of her legs at
    the café when she crosses and uncrosses them. The almost-hidden
    sound of her swishing hose.
But the flick of her wrist. The way she butters her croissant while
    pouting her lower lip, as if it were the touch and lather that mattered.

Tell her I have been abroad.

Remind her of the equatorial heat with which I have returned from the depth of descent. An imaginary graph of the roundness of now. The swirl and twirl of the earth's girth.

The Inconsolable Study of Iron

Now we return to the study of iron.
We come as bracelets. We come as train cars coupling the dark.

Bury a bowl of Armenian apples beside the track.
Do not switch their stems with veins in your wrist.

Once, when I was six, I killed something extraordinarily precious.
I will forever, and might not, but could if fevered just right.

You confiscate my mouth and whisper the phrase *Little boy playing*
   tenderly with an ant, grant me the sad safe hair of the willow.
I wriggle and turn. I shake and shed. I caress everything dear yet piercing
   as if I were bait on a hook.

Whatever you do, don't try to convince me of the advantage of the iron
   content of my blood.
Someone arrived secretly in the night, stole the salt, and in its place left
   only a milk snake that twitches whenever I try to cull the moon. To
   call it down into my throat. To blurt the urge of the ever-shifting earth
   of the not-quite-dead.

Echopraxia

So Valentine Penrose was secretly dating Alice Rahon.
My book of proverbs was secretly dating me.

I began each morning with finger exercises I had learned from a piano
   teacher in Luxor.
There was strength in the desert. The symphonic march for a few shade
   trees and clear well water.

There seemed always something to be said for the unsaid.
Spoken there, on the sheets beneath us, were the imprints of the
   constant cravings of birds.

Sparrow secretions, you once said, into my shy and embarrassed ear.
And I heard the world break apart every time our tongues touched
   lightning in the folds folded into sleep.

So André Breton was not so secretly dating Lise Deharme.
Even as his wife, Simone Kahn, was secretly pleading to me.

Which meant I'd once lived in a poem inside the desk drawer of Paul
   Éluard.
And Upper Volta flowed south into the Nile that somehow kept flowing
   to Athens, Andalusia, and me.

And the clarinet that was given unto me was actually a piano, not a
   bassoon.
And each note I worked to finger in the dark somehow remained intact,
   year after year, life upon life—pleading plaintively its elegant swan
   notes back unto me.

Falling for Lee Miller in a Previous Incarnation in Which We Never Became Lovers

One woman, stylishly dressed, holding a demitasse cup, sipping Turkish
    coffee.
Her eyes belonged to that hidden hole in my heart.

I fell madly in love with a photograph of her elegantly stitched clothes in
    a pile on the floor.
As for her shoes, I could only hope she'd still wear them, even tromp in
    them, otherwise naked among an ink-spill of leaves.

In those days, I would have been alarmed by the objectifying of my own
    wrist clock.
Always fashionable, she knew nothing was as pronounced as a quiet
    portrait in black and white.

And when I finally caught sight of her, we looked at each other—one
    unclad instant—each wondering, I imagined, whether we'd survive
    the reliquary of our own breathing.
Didn't that glimpsed breath, after all, bring us closer to the pulsing seed?

In those days, I knew Man Ray, peripherally, not just as *Emmanuel* but as
    Man.
On his arm at the theater, would she be called *Elegant Blonde Heron?*
    Most Pleasant View of Poughkeepsie? Or *His Woman Somehow*
    Hovering Near My Chest?

Back then, I was incredibly shy, touching others only in my private dark,
   certain the wagon circle and lantern dance somehow represented the
   nomadic parts of my heart.
That the fires she and I both moved around—each in separate worlds—
   never ceased.

If We Wanted to Coax the Crows

Even though twilight is not just evening but also the time between
complete darkness and sunrise, it still seemed odd to say we ate our
morning oats at twilight.
However, if we wanted to coax crows to fly back through our open
holes, we knew we had to become more open-minded.

That's not a joke.
Consider poems that transcend poetry and conjure termites from the
voice of Him or Her who has always been with us. The one we most
love.

For many years I kept a cabin in a remote area of my brain.
I slung a lantern there every night when I took to the woods and
followed the hounds.

It took me decades before I felt comfortable enough to eat a dictionary
for breakfast.
Cutlets were the easiest. Frying up slabs of words so I might safely get
through my day. Uncharmed.

I especially loved when my grandmother would feed the cookstove and
make cornmeal mush into a magical adventure of glorious golden
brown.
All the world's pans might flour my mouth in ways that would never
scald or stick.

Careful, I knew, not to extend a metaphor beyond plausible deniability.
Where were you the night of the fifth? I heard beneath the glaring lamp.
*And what wind passed through your open throat, claiming only to be
searching for me?*

Ex Libris

I knew the way home oddly enough through a close examination of her
    bookplates.
I'd remove several books from her shelves, across categories—
    Astronomy, Hunting, Poetry, Gauguin in the South Seas—somehow
    mapping my way back.

Each bookplate, pasted onto the books' boards, contained pictures,
    words, even a lock of her hair.
Stubborn sassafras grew in the backyard, enhancing my ill mood.

Exasperation as a form of our most human confusion?
The tired trails of termites and ants as an answer to how to survive what
    most eats us from below?

I think I told you she liked to read?
I likely mentioned that when her neighbor's hamster left the body, it
    rained and rained and kept raining golden leaves from the trees?
    Bendings from the willows?

Still, there it was below the sycamore and honeysuckle drawings on her
    bookplates: her perfect signature as inexplicably cautious as the most
    considerate winds.
Each letter of her name somehow calling forth the sun-browned belly of
    the moon.

Poker comes to mind—always betting against itself. And jai alai. And
    miniature golf with the agonizing turn of those windmills.
Myths are like that. And gobbling Chinese takeout straight from the box.
    And dental fillings without Novocain. And death.

Wrong Side of the Body

Crushed by wind, by the amatory birds, my heart of long-asleep bees is
  celestial ascent.
Let me put it this way: I am finally alive.

I see how the sleep sickness in Uganda was caused by a fly.
There are docile moments when even children of divorce survive.

Details conspire. Interrupt the flow of personal yet purposeful.
Let the language go wonky, let it fracture, let it urgent, even without
  torn parts of the heart.

Still, we break apart into one another.
The depth of your hand on my chest is extra ordinary.

Let us forsake the bridge between words.
Let us forsake convention and simultaneously *both* be on top.

Measureless hour of paradoxical tongue-thought, dissolved now in the
  crankshaft of a kōan.
There is extreme monotony in knowing you are right.

A solitary part of my scar has fallen in love with another more remote
  scar—from the wrong side of the body—had to get married, had a
  baby, even a couple more, and is now suffering from inbreeding
  various cuts and scuffs from only one side of the tracks.
Oh, God—did I just say *that*? It must be the scar speaking *of* me,
  through me, with or without the permission of my long-hurt heart.

The Mamzelles of Copenhagen

In order to be presentable, I asked several women I had not previously
known to water-comb my hair.
In those days, the mail arrived but every third month. And I was
desperate for connection.

There was a sick cow named Astrid lying in the barn. Or was she
Annalena? She was as wise and beautiful as the blowing wind of her
name.
I spent my days worrying over her, spearing freshwater eels in the river,
trying to ignore the dark dents that captured my concern.

Yes, wood mice clung like vines to my mood.
Seaweed beckoned and sank my blood among bladderwrack and
badderlocks.

Not even the mamzelles of Copenhagen could ease my tension, much of
which had to do with a worried cow and her bellowing calf.
Not even the mute swans and mallards. Nor the owl on fire in the
kerosene lamps.

Absorbed among sea thong and foam, I began platting my bones as if
they were prayer beads or moon-absorbed stones.
I asked after the ship's captain. Could he somehow calm the animal's
suffering from afar? Grant me a current of almost-solid air? A kind
gesture that might one day rid me of my skin and guide the lantern
light—from the drifting barns of my past—ashore?

Blister Me, If You Must, with Poetic Side-Eye

At that time, we had left Zhangjiakou by oxcart, taking the road roughly
   toward Dajingmen Pass.
Mud-roofed huts. Dilapidated inns. The Swedish mission at Gulchaggan.

Lord knows I spent yet another incarnation in complete and utter
   distress.
I don't care if I write flat lines. If I say too little too much. Feel free to
   blister me with poetic side-eye.

When you leave a little buttered tea in the bottom of your bowl, know
   you are only mimicking a moment of loss.
Until the Mekong extends into an ethnological province, a river of
   bridges will keep splintering into the ever-flowing dead.

Dream this. Dream that. The clangor of cymbals. Our heartache bowing
   before the butterlamps burning on the altar.
Honestly. I wanted a normal life this time, though I didn't quite know
   what that meant or how.

Brief yourself in the subsequent of your mirror.
Study the reticulated grains of a ritual glance.

I once got a glimpse of a partial tantra drained of the inner lives of owls.
I could slip away into the trees of depleted apprenticeship and believe
   that reading books on wood mice might require the proclamation of a
   new canon.

A Spectacular Grievance of Inverted Rain

In any instant, it could be a bluegill or a green sunfish of the southern
    swamp country.
Even my friends told me I needed to get out more, to forget the dip of its
    swim, the grip of nighthawks in my chest.

Even Mary Ann was adamant. But there was a spectacular grievance of
    inverted rain.
There were bog conditions inside me, sphagnum in my throat.

And so since the season was very much a stretch of late August, we
    knew we were locked in the summer of a small lake.
And when the little sedges revealed crocodile tail inscriptions of nightly
    dreams we'd told to no one, we were certain the gnawing of a
    porcupine in an aspen grove was just a cautionary music.

It must have been my three-day beard that startled me.
I was suddenly gray, top to bottom, yet whenever I stumbled upon a
    mirror I felt I was getting further from the truth.

Born in winter, as a child of the cold, I woke each morning longing to see
    the snowshoe hare.
I vowed to clear the snow on my back steps then walk up and down
    them continuously for an hour, seeing if I could catch the falling flakes
    on my tongue before they melted, hoping the way they dissolved
    inside me might teach me to love seeing myself walking away from
    what others were constantly fleeing toward.

We Wore Monk Hair

The Galaxies' True Forms Expand

Off in my head the way a book.
Down through my heart if I but could.

Pavlina, we might go wet inside.
I might find of you and tumble and plead.

What angel talk might the coffee grinder consider?
What *You-are-dark-where-I-most-hurt* might we most beautifully youth?

There was a front and a back.
That is all we knew of prayer-dimensional space.

Which meant we hadn't yet gone deeply enough.
On my knees, kissing every inch of your skin, the whole universe
    expands.

The fear of complete nakedness is nothing when one sits in meditation
    each morning and evening to burn off the karmic seeds and their
    accumulated ache and age.
I'll brackish my water and fand of you my mouth.

Idiomize me.
Diphthong my heart.

Off to the side, the way a past life might quietly glimpse us.
Up through the spine, as if. No, *not* "as if" —*this*, the galaxies' true
    forms expand.

Good, Bad, Indifferent

And heal me. And say my name sadly as you might the torn texture of
plankton.
Do you believe in a proper look? Would you kiss me even if I was not
composed of starlight?

There have been many incarnations in which I did not believe in
incarnations.
None of which can be taken back, just as the body is not able to douse
fire.

We may be compared to India's first moon.
We may require blood sockets, the sleet of a dragonfly to guide our
blistering summer mouths.

I have tried everything, and I have tried nothing.
To live a life of love would be a great good gain.

It is no longer possible to dissect green into haves and have-nots.
I can now tell who is secretly the color blue.

When Lord Krishna awoke in my chest, I knew everything I'd hoped to
lose.
A bit of spit, a spate of quail blood, and I'm back on my feet no matter
what they might display.

There's something sudden, and there's something clumsy in all they say I
do.
We must awake in these plants at our feet and ask whether they
understand the directional shrift of breath.

A bowl of moonlight clocks the cold acres of the sky.
Good, bad, indifferent. It is all here, on the table, before me.

The Sinking Gray Beds of Gravel

The deeper issue was that things in Japan sank. The ground swelled out
and fell deeper into itself.
It would behoove us to consider the various uses of wasabi and ginger in
board games like Shogi and Go. How fraught it became to both win
and lose.

True, the hillfolk of the Appalachians believed they should not boast or
put on airs, boiling ramps and collards at their cookstoves.
In the backwoods of nearly every man and woman of the world lies at
least one really terrible haircut.

If you ask me, well, you ask me.
Gather ye questions while ye may.

I decided to give up teaching, so I could learn to sing harmonious shape
notes in the hill country.
I bought every volume of *Firefox* available, but the only instruction I
could find was how to build a dulcimer, butcher a hog, or glimpse the
ghastliness of a woods-bound ghost.

Our hearts sank.
And every cliché fell further into the earth.

Sweet music of unavoidable death.
Many of us from Chicago's South Side had good Greek blood but
believed Alexander should not have continued on into India.

Yes, there were yearly famines and epidemics in those mountains.
Princely kingdoms waiting to crumble. Everything falling through
everything else as the world was beginning to breathe.
But centuries later when I lived in Kyoto there were temples with
gorgeous Zen gardens. Celibate rakes that shaped the most beautiful
swirls in the otherwise sinking gray beds of gravel.

Ghost Offering

The midnight drift of Dakota and the hungry boreal.
The fogbank, poleward, of a desolate thought.

There is a spectral moon twenty miles from the wobbling freight of a
train.
Hazy horizons thicken as if there will never be an adequate explanation.

It was an idiot sea of wheat that wrinkled my beard, though not-yet-
grown.
The limbo of a recalcitrant match case was left raked by the fingers of a
cruel north wind.

Let us create and recreate the roar of a jealous cure.
The sea launched a thousand sunsets. The waves were golden as
blackbirds' wings named *Helen.*

It was the fleet loneliness of a flickering dark.
The pause, as if with the eye it could have all been ours.

What did a simple Badlands explanation ultimately have to do with stars
cutting through a floaty fog?
We secured all there was to breathe—so that no one could swell the
horizon with a monotone suspicion from across the sea—giving us a
ghostly offering in Dakota. All the way from Takamatsu. From the
Kalahari hills. From dust storms in Algiers and the mineral rinse of
Malta.

From wind in the stiff sails of the throat.
A bitter yet necessary exhalation.

This Body, This Reliquary of Bone

Shall I ask my startled breath how many species of starlings have settled
    into it?
Shall I relinquish and roam and reliquary?

There was lassitude. Laxity. Listlessness.
It wasn't just that the wind had abandoned our sails.

That was, of course, the lifetime I took to water.
Oh, how in scouring the midnight stars I had believed I could swim
    through anything.

You say the compass point of my mouth is wrong. That I require your
    emphatic direction.
You speak like an equilibrist, tightrope walking through my many moods.

There was an eremic desire, even after years of sea salt.
There were strange sounds burbling up through us, as if the dead from
    all the sea.

Caliginous hour of the tongue.
Dark noun obscuring my mouth.

We were born this time, I tell you, because we *needed* to be born.
Sunlight—disguised as moonshadow—entered then settled into a grove
    of palms bent of salt, seeming to weep as they strained to embrace
    me.

I Refuse to Let You Plan My Past

I've read of the disrespect of others. Felt the shunning in this whisper
  and that.
I've seen some people place a house thermometer into a deer's leg,
  probing for 160 degrees of good health and hope.

There is salt in quantity too. Blankets of it in the chonky waves. Piles of
  history the sea exudes.
We employ delicate words as we tongue-touch and blur into the skin of
  another.

I kept lamenting my sorry lot—my two arms juggling the memory of a
  trio of Tasmanian pears.
Everything I'd wanted to say had been far away. A tree snake, I'd
  learned, was nothing more than a perpetual perplexity.

I refuse the alphabet of a rickshaw moon, wheel upon wheel grinding
  out onto the cobblestone a new vowel.
I fall back into my past and remember subterfuge and sweat.

The ultimate trap is to exist apart from tree rings going round and round
  in the Saturn-turn of calm reunion?
We become birth stars and slurp back the dying exhalation of our own
  fiery breath?

When the mailman knocked on the door, I had a true sense of purpose.
  Even importance.
It was finally spring. There were documents to read, signatures to sign,
  all while the cardinal at the window bestowed upon me the brilliant
  red renewal of jewels.

Great Deeps

Her body desired proof of his voice.
His mouth relinquished remnants of rain.

Her universe seemed to make the most fortunate sound.
His tongue found the curve of her scar.

Over the centuries, the skin of fingers derives great deeps.
The chthonic alphabet is barely visible in sound waves buried in the
    bulbous tuft of bone.

To get down on our knees and welcome the majority of our words.
To ask if the letters come *before* the utterance. Or the utterance before
    the rain.

Meanwhile, I am lovingly behind my radiance.
I am bent into the dream in which—letting my body go—I lean backward
    into the dark for balance, not self-blame.

When I woke, we all woke into the dogs around us.
They were asleep on sofas, on cedar beds, on wood-warmed rugs, as if
    fully awake, practicing point on a star.

The Book of Substitute Flesh as Revealed in The Book of Exaggerated Salt

It is written in *The Book of Substitute Flesh* that once we experience loss
we tend only to want to read excerpts from *The Book of Refracted
Starlight.*
Follow the droplets in *The Book of Hard Rain*; they will guide you to *The
Book of Confiscated Sea Salt.*

As a child I read everything, fascinated most with *The Book of Bent
Trees.*
Later, I came to see every woman in the world as part of *The Book of
Slow Willows by the River.*

After morning meditation, it felt as if my skin had not yet fully grown
back.
I looked for it, stunned, inside *The Book of How Might I and When?*

Then my voice arrived from afar.
It came from centuries past, as if Odysseus had cared for it in a leather
pouch all those beard years at sea.

I wanted to make love to the grass, the plants, even to the rose of
Sharon in the backyard.
But how I might and when truly confused me.

I sensed answers would reside in *The Book of the Owl on Fire in My
Chest.*
I knew that was only one volume, though, within the encyclopedic *The
Book of Kerosene Lamps.*

All my favorite books were there. Alphabetized by the second word of
each title.
All my substitute selves finally arrived and seemed to grovel as they
gathered around me.

I sat alphabetizing, far too confused how to order the long line of my
reading beginning with each title's second word: *Book* this, say, and
Book that.
Then came the river prior to its pockmarking rain. And I became
engrossed all evening in the pestering pages of *The Book of Mayflies
Disguised as Deranged Gnats*—knowing I was meant to blur
boundaries of words and read myself into the reeds, the sea, the
depths of me.

Were We Sad?

The repression of a baroque illumination is very plainly archetypal.
The artistic birth of Carl Jung exceeds all expectation.

For where there is insufficient art, the fly wing in the ear of a sow is
    emblematic.
It is not about listening but about the way rain falls apart.

As if Brahms were a relative.
As if Brahms, damp, on a late September porch, taught me how to
    speak.

Summer has suddenly ended.
Our breath is visible, our insides on ice.

There is something amazing in the time structure of a book.
First we are born, and then we become another, making love not only
    with our body, but drifting through the night sky of our partner's star.

Generate more duplication of damp clay, and we have a body for every
    necessary rebirth.
Spin forth from the Great Wheel and see what imprints of eels scrape
    off, ecstatic, into our mud.

The metaphorical, almost ineffable, puzzlement pleasantly inscribes the
    haptic nerve with which we are left.
Were we happy? Were we sad? Of course—we were human,
    circumambulating the fire ants, stroking the char of each electric
    birth. The char of our flower-bitten bones biting the scar of yet
    another chance to be truly alive.

How Beautiful the Cut

Not how beautiful the cut tree could be.
Nor the core conceit of a poem's dissolve.

Not the utmost throat, the eels finally releasing an internal pillar of fire
    in the deaf man's ear.
Certainly not the word *not* knotted up in knocking the knotty pine walls
    of our youth precisely three and one-third times.

Not the bell and constabulary of Bolivia, the yanggona excursion to Fiji.
Never the utmost nor of the throat, lonely in the kingdom of spat leaves.

Not the fiber nest secreted in the priest's cloak—not so comfortable as it
    looks.
Nor the lace-trimmed eggs of the tortoise, ocean meat sweeter than a
    cadre of ants.

But the word *but*. No, not even that buttress of caution arching
    sideways, epistolary braid against this line of mind.
Certainly not bees breaking the brain of its entire cold phrase, nor the
    scent-driven verve of *and*, *so*, and even *nor*.

Let me be clear: Nothing exists in the words *Nothing exists.*
Not even in the phrase *The beautiful cut hair of a monk, shaved and*
    facing east each morning, wakes most lovingly in the aching moon-
    threads of sleep.

A Room of Quite Ripe Weeping

When the new year begins, what do we bring into it from Van Gogh's
    discarded left earlobe?
Show me how the organ grinder rotates the planets in my chest, and I'll
    calculate the number of times my skin has cried out for touch.

The procession of delighted weepings set out across the vast Colorado
    plains in search of water to renew those tears.
If I set myself to read a superior adventure novel, would it be enriched
    by a frightening African landscape? A fish-beached moon snagged in
    the branches of a baobab?

When you first visit a cemetery grounds, you are taken to a room of
    quite ripe weeping.
Not a room, exactly, but a thicket of gallberries and quivering sparrows.

Nothing tonight but the dead weight of death.
Nothing but a clot of camphor waiting in the child's fist to clog the sea.

These features are only a few remnants you encounter near the
    Kankakee or Wabash. Even in the bones of a fish washed up from the
    Bay of Bengal.
I knew that if I was handed a dead starling and asked to make soup, I
    must first make certain to allow it time to recompose the sky onto the
    vast retina of its unblinking eye.

Sometimes I Cried

That I might heal like this.
That I might be strong like something wounded but calm.

And so at last the animals I wept ignored me, urging me in their silence
    to walk away.
Instead of gold, water dripped from the cabin roof beneath a covey of
    alder and birch.

A great many mouths were competing for my voice. For *this* threat of
    sound, for *that*?
They made squealing noises, as if fallen into the bamboo-spiked pits of
    hunters.

Then autumn called. There were slitherings of mud like sea snakes
    sunning themselves.
Sometimes I cried—living so close as I was to drift and bone.

Then a snarling from behind a tree. A sharpening of claws.
And the pileated moon somehow got swallowed by the clouds becoming
    more fully themselves.

But the dark sky all those years was almost worth it, opening holes
    within the holes therein.
I have lived so many lives, it would be wonderful, finally—when the time
    comes—to fly out of this body, becoming a bird.

I Wore Monk Hair

It's the story of three quarrelling mountains.
She stayed up, drinking oolong tea, reading late into the night.

It's the story of the lust and sound, of the boxwood comb located and
    prized, even now, in our century.
She had presented the crown prince with the pure white of an orange
    blossom.

It's a story as familiar as the fin-flash of koi.
How my chest aches for that flurry, that blur, for that brilliant black on
    gold.

There's a light, still, twelve centuries later, in my throat.
I do not exaggerate when I ask you to keep the lantern lit with the
    purest kerosene, the most moist lice, drawn from the blubber of a
    walrus far to the north.

A long time ago, I wandered the woods near Nishitomi Hills.
I wore monk hair, ate nothing but shitake mushroom broth, and—on
    occasion—sat by my river reflection waiting for oceanic monkfish to
    pass through it, back and forth, as if I weren't already alive.

Notes

Epigraphs

André Breton: The first Breton quote is from *Manifesto of Surrealism* (1924), and the second is from *Soluble Fish* (1924). Both are translated by Richard Seaver and Helen R. Lane, from *Manifestoes of Surrealism*, University of Michigan Press, 1972.

W.S. Merwin: This quote is from "The Current," in *Writings to an Unfinished Accompaniment*, Atheneum, 1976.

Eleni Vakalo: This quote comes from a response to one painting in a series by Giorgos Vakalo. Each painting is accompanied by a line of poetry by his wife, poet Eleni Vakalo, translated by Philip Ramp, from *A day with fish, animals and birds* [*sic*] ("published on the occasion of the one man [*sic*] show of G. Vakalo at the Ora Athens Cultural Center, March 1971"), Ora Athens Cultural Center, 1971.

Textual Notes

In "Initial Me as You Would," the first sentence of the closing stanza ("O great teacher of Japanese bedlam") echoes Wallace Stevens from "Thirteen Ways of Looking at a Blackbird," section VII (which begins "O thin men of Haddam"), as I echo not only his phrasing but also sound (i.e., "bedlam" and "Haddam"), from *The Collected Poems of Wallace Stevens*, Alfred A. Knopf, 1957.

In "Such Is the Play of Light Within Silkworm Ephemera," a few phrases are taken from *Mirages on the Sea of Time: The Taoist Poetry of Ts'ao T'ang*, Edward H. Schafer, University of California Press, 1985.

"The Immortal Abode of the Nine Ancients" and "Evening Bell at the Holy Monastery" borrow their titles from two poems by Guo Mruo, from his book

Famous Mountain of the World, Emei Shan (publisher), Leshan, Sichuan Province, China, 1980.

The title "Eight Hundred Vultures Feeding on a Dead Horse" comes from the description of a photograph in William Beebe's *Pheasant Jungles*, G. P. Putnam Sons, 1927. Stanza two is a near verbatim rendering from this book (an image description, along with a phrase from the main text).

"The Studio of True Appreciation" takes its title from the title of a Ming Dynasty painting by Wen Zhengming, reproduced in the magazine *Global Tea Hut*, issue devoted to "Tea Spaces," Summer 2023.

The poem "The Hero's Journey" takes its title from Joseph Campbell's *The Hero's Journey: Joseph Campbell on His Life and Work*, New World Library, 2014.

In "Wind Within Wind Within the Way Trees Bend," "Aegean Melancholy" is the title of a famous poem by Odysseus Elytis, and the *moon that rose from the sea like Aphrodite* is a line from an equally famous poem by George Seferis. These are from Odysseus Elytis, *Selected Poems*, chosen and introduced by Edmund Keeley and Philip Sherrard, translation of this poem by the same, the Viking Press and Penguin Books, 1981, and George Seferis, "Helen," from *Collected Poems*, expanded edition, translated, edited, and introduced by Edmund Keeley and Philip Sherrard, Princeton University Press, 1981.

In "Good, Bad, Indifferent," the title and subsequent repetition of this phrase later in the poem is an approximation of a quote from Swami Kriyananda's audio lectures *Lessons in Yoga: 14 Steps to Higher Awareness*, Crystal Clarity Publishers, 1989.

The authorship of other occasional quotations in this book should hopefully be clear from the various contexts in which these quotations appear.

Selected Poetry Titles Published by SurVision Books

Contemporary Tangential Surrealist Poetry: An Anthology
Edited by Tony Kitt
ISBN 978-1-912963-44-7

Invasion: An Anthology of Ukrainian Poetry about the War
Edited by Tony Kitt
ISBN 978-1-912963-32-4

Noelle Kocot. *Humanity*
(New Poetics: USA)
ISBN 978-1-9995903-0-7

Marc Vincenz. *Einstein Fledermaus*
(New Poetics: USA)
ISBN 978-1-912963-20-1

Helen Ivory. *Maps of the Abandoned City*
(New Poetics: England)
ISBN 978-1-912963-04-1

Tony Kitt. *The Magic Phlute*
(New Poetics: Ireland)
ISBN 978-1-912963-08-9

Mikko Harvey & Jake Bauer. *Idaho Falls*
(Winner of James Tate Poetry Prize 2018)
ISBN 978-1-912963-02-7

John Bradley. *Spontaneous Mummification*
(Winner of James Tate Poetry Prize 2019)
ISBN 978-1-912963-13-3

Charles Kell. *Pierre Mask*
(Winner of James Tate Poetry Prize 2019)
ISBN 978-1-912963-19-5

Charles Borkhuis. *Spontaneous Combustion*
(Winner of James Tate Poetry Prize 2021)
ISBN 978-1-912963-30-0

Noah Falck and Matt Mcbride. *Prerecorded Weather*
(Winner of James Tate Poetry Prize 2022)
ISBN 978-1-912963-39-3

Jeffrey Cyphers Wright. *Fuel for Love*
(Winner of James Tate Poetry Prize 2023)
ISBN 978-1-912963-45-4

George Kalamaras. *That Moment of Wept*
ISBN 978-1-9995903-7-6

George Kalamaras. *Through the Silk-Heavy Rains*
ISBN 978-1-912963-28-7

Ciaran O'Driscoll. *Angel Hour*
ISBN 978-1-912963-27-0

Guillaume Apollinaire. *Ocean of Earth: Selected Poems*
Translated from French by Matthew Geden
ISBN 978-1-912963-40-9

Anton G. Leitner. *Selected Poems 1981–2015*
Translated from German
ISBN 978-1-9995903-8-3

Order our books from survisionmagazine.com

www.ingramcontent.com/pod-product-compliance
Lightning Source LLC
LaVergne TN
LVHW021553080426

835510LV00019B/2495